Shadow Work Fall 2024

a poetry anthology

Edited by
Cat Speranzini & Matthew Pasquarello

Copyright © 2024

Grey Coven Publishing
Instagram: @greycovenpublishing
greycovenpublishing@gmail.com

Cover by Cat Speranzini using Canva

ISBN # 9798218495220

Contents

"I bloom in the
shadows."

- *nataša benedičič*

The Man I Don't Recognize – Zack Albertini

I looked in the mirror and didn't recognize the man I saw. Crimson eyes from sleepless nights and one too many sips of alcohol. There're grays in his beard now, but surely he's too young for that. Crow's feet perched upon his eyes, receding hair hidden by his hat. The bags under his eyes look like he splurged at the mall. His skin looks tired, ragged, and ready to fall. Weight fluctuates, scars punctuate, all these things hide the mind he can't escape. Because if there was a mirror to the mind, you'd see the kind of flaws he wouldn't want you to find. A growing list of goals he can't seem to attain, depression racking his brain, a hunger for more from which he just can't abstain. He just can't obtain anything besides pain. Anything besides sadness, and more come to claim. But still, he looks in the mirror, unrecognizable to me. And still, I fight for him, and all he wants to be.

On metamorphosis - Nataša Benedičič

I slide my hand down my rib cage, to feel
the power of life pulsing underneath. My thoughts
flow like a river through my body. Everything
I once felt still lives inside of me. I can hear
the echo of my ancestors in my lungs. I can taste
the innate wisdom inside my bones. I've been
a caterpillar many times, still I am not done.
Stardust colouring my wings. True nature of
love is in flowingness, you don't fight it,
you don't go against it; you let it wreak havoc
in the chambers of your heart. In the aftermath
you'll learn to fly once more, with new wings.

Inkling - Nataša Benedičič

There was an inkling somewhere deep in my rib cage,
someone important will someday cross my path.
 I've lived with it for years, until unexpectedly
our eyes met and you untangled my heart
to its truest form. The feeling of coming
home pierced my soul, as if we were
tied together. Ancient flowers in
my bones are blooming, yet
this feeling is my own,
and I water it
in silence.

I bloom in the shadows - Nataša Benedičič

I bloom in the shadows
away from the blinding sun
I turn to where no one else follows
my roots digging into the soil for secrets written
finding peace in a land forgotten

Beauty found in sadness - Nataša Benedičič

Piano notes lingering in my
lonesome heart, like gentle
raindrops hugging my skin
I walk down the path and
let myself feel it all, until
my soul is soaked through
and through; admiring
the beauty found in sadness
with an open heart, it finds
a home inside, but I
leave the door open.

Castaway – Michelle Bosonnett

My mind is a thunderstorm,
My body a shipwreck, thrashed and
Desecrated by hands of hate.
I am a castaway.
I have wrestled monsters in the deepest dark,
Feigned hopeful smiles in castigation of daylight.
My chaos was born of tyrannic hunger.
My constellations light the night sky.
Can you see me from here?
I lull in a void of vast emptiness,
Merging with the ocean.
Sea creatures feast on the rot of my bones.
I cannot capture the sun.
I drift in an abyss of dark sorrow;
nobody is coming to save me.
Nobody can hear my pleas for mercy; my voice is too
meek.
I need no one but me.
I am shapeshifting, slowly morphing, transforming.
My oceanic eyes can drown volcanic mountains.
I will breathe fire, roar,
Take the heat from the stars.
I will birth myself in this confusion of doom,
I will love myself back to life.
I will run with the moon,
Atalantic, euphoric, heroic
In my true form.

Anatomy of a Scream – Michelle Bosonnett

Of all the sounds my body is capable of,
My scream is the most lethal.
It is silent, a violent silence, a deafening silence.
It is a guttural vibration that shakes my brain,
A modulation of sound so profound
It shatters the sky.
It screeches and claws behind my eyes.
It flaps and scratches against my cries
And sends shockwaves flying deep into the earth.
Gypsum, violet and red tempered,
Its viridian edges and stark white lead
Dizzy my mind and paralise my limbs with dread.
It drains the colour from my face and
Laces with the merging night.
My scream is black barbed wire,
Dire and bloodied in my throat.
It unleashes hell and laughs as I choke.
It culls the words I need to speak and
Renders me depleted, fatigued, weak.
My scream is silent.
Silent, lethal and violent.

"I will birth myself in this confusion of doom, I will love myself back to life."

- *Michelle Bosonnett*

An Intervention – Morgan Bridges

I.

I have never thought of myself as an addict. but I dwell in
a dangerous place between obsession and hyperfixation.

> Each time I recount story upon story,
> I circle back through a worn-out collection. I
> have traversed the eroded territory of my
> brain and picked up shards of memory
> along the way and jammed them at their
> edges. I prayed they would finally fit
> together.

II.

5 years old: Daddy fell off the wagon
 and crashed the whole damn thing.
7 years old: Sissy weighs less than I do,
and I don't know why she isn't hungry.
10 years old: I don't really remember this,
 and maybe it's better that way.
12 years old: Mama was diagnosed
with breast cancer, but she tells me not to worry.
13 years old: Daddy's nine lives finally ran out;
the nursing home said he expired.

These are the small white pills in my grasp,
clutched to my chest like precious stones.
Take away my pen, and my hands begin
to tremble and shake. Leave me idle, and I will trudge
through them again, finding another way to explain and
over-explain.
I will find synonyms for *fucked up* that

I haven't used before. I will unveil a detail that is so earth-
shattering, it'll be like watching a trainwreck in motion.
Too grotesque to look away. Let me tell my story one
more time.

I promise it'll be different.

III.

I promise there was some good, some less tragic, within
the years I've lived.
I'll have to let you know when I remember them.
It'd be nice to have the luxury of therapy
and reclaim the years before I turned 13 —
the years he was still here.

For now, those years, feel like memories
on a beaten movie reel, glimpses of truth
that don't feel like mine. I feel like I am
telling someone else's story.

IV.

I'm not a one-trick horse. I have this itch that needs to be
scratched. This insatiable urge to regurgitate the same tale
until I am sick of it myself. Maybe I am more of a one-
track mind, and maybe that makes me more like my
grandmother, my father, and my sister. Maybe I am
doomed to continue tradition.

They wanted to feel something.
They wanted to leave their present and find solace
amongst the clouds.
They didn't want to hurt anymore.

I don't either.

19

V.

I just find my high in different places,
the adrenaline of knowing the truth.

Vulnerability – Morgan Bridges

When he saw my bare skin for the first time,
I wanted to disappear, fade into nothingness.
The warmth of his brown eyes

singed my skin, and I didn't know how
to formulate the words:
please, look away. His lips formed

a small, appreciative smile as he complimented my
curves. I didn't know how to tell him how much

I wanted to take scissors and cut away
every part of me that I hated.

Peel myself back, layer by layer. Becoming smaller
until I felt I was someone he could love. I slipped

his XL shirt over too-broad shoulders and his smile
 deepened. Dimples exposed. I didn't know how to

explain that my reflection was my deepest fear.
How could I hate the very thing he loved?

Vulnerability pt. II – Morgan Bridges

Overweight. Overwhelming. Overwrought.

I exist in a list of excess, simultaneously too much and never quite enough. I couldn't fit into the box he wanted to put me in, no matter how much I crammed and squeezed and shimmied. I will burst out of its coarse edges every time, slicing soft flesh on his expectations. I can't remember the last time his eyes wandered over my body, lingered on the warmth of my eyes or the subtle blush of my cheeks, and muttered: "You're beautiful." Instead, he watched the crimson slide down my sides and the length of my legs, puddling slowly at my feet. In the darkened reflection, I saw a multitude of double texts, a constant plea for reassurance, and failed attempts at bringing the loneliness to its end. My silhouette didn't feel like mine, morphed and unrecognizable. Always does. His eyes looked directly through me, and I could sense the amount of space I stole away in the confines of my room. Somehow he still charmed his way into my skin.

I've never felt so small.

A letter I will never send – Morgan Bridges

I don't remember the first time we met face to face, if I'm
being honest
No, no, I assure you you've made an impression on me –
like a scar that lingers but doesn't completely fade.
You're etched into my skin. *Can't you see?*

     My lip's bleeding, and my cuticles are ravaged.

I know you didn't mean to. My idle hands just picked and
picked,
tearing away small bits of myself, searching aimlessly for
the kind of pain that reminds me I exist.
I wonder if I'll find you there instead,

               burrowed near my smile or sleeping
               soundly in my nail beds.

I've always second-guessed the words uttered from this
mouth.
Never thought these hands would create anything – much
less extraordinary.
That was you, *wasn't it?* I'm probably getting a little
ahead of myself.
Accusations don't really make friends, do they?

       I want to believe we were once just that.

Back when you were filled with good intention, you'd
keep me safe.
You'd keep me tucked away under your arm, holding me
close so I
wouldn't wander astray. You'd pull me back from the
ledge, instead of pushing me over it
without a second glance.

Instead, you smirk as I spiral down and down and down.

The image is as woven into the fabric of my mind as you
are.
You've infiltrated mundane moments and injected them
with chaos,
made routine obsessive. You've illustrated cruel pictures
of worst-case scenarios
and tucked them in the recesses of my brain for
safekeeping.

Why must you torture me so?

Check the candle three times or it wasn't blown out.
The door's only closed if it's locked. If the door is left
open,
my dog will leave too. My dog is my only family three
hours from home.
You constantly remind me he won't live forever.

Hell, you've even made me believe I was dying. Vision
filled with spots
and head swimming – drowning. You stole the breath
from my lungs and forced
my heart to pound double-time. My roommate's voice
yelled over yours,
Morgan, you're having a panic attack.

Was our meeting fate simply destined from the moment I
was born?
Dad may have introduced us unintentionally, but Mom
warned me about you–
too little, too late. I wish I knew how to fix the mess
you've made of me.
I wish you didn't make me feel broken, a screw loose in
my brain

Oh, Anxiety, how I despise you.

I've learned how to steady my breathing, focus
on the world around me, and I swear I'll find my escape.
I'll dance out of your clutches smiling,
free at last,
and I'll bid you a fond farewell.

"I didn't know how to explain that my reflection was my deepest fear."

- *Morgan Bridges*

FROM THE VOID WE CAME (and to the void we must return) – Prudence Brooks

A key-notched corpse walking cold in the nettles; thorns
prick my marred and pallid flesh. A crescent light hangs
just over the horizon, gesturing towards the water
Like a shepherd. Like a guide.

The moon's reflection on the river
makes gravity seem heavier,
marks everything a bit more grave.
Meowing ravens materialize above,
gathering in groups among the naked branches.

In my mind, birds have always been proof that the
most beautiful things
are also the most terrifying.
I have always known
they are a beacon though.
I am so, so close.

I can feel relief already in my throat,
bubbling like a Big Red soda.
Tasting of corn syrup and old comforts. I am afraid
but I am even more exhilarated, delighted for what's
next.

(as in the nothingness.)

I finally reach the rocky riverbed
and slip off my grubby canvas sneakers. I take a
careful step into the water,
bitterly frigid and thrilling in its sharpness. I keep
wading, waist deep,

and in a flash of freshwater and light, I am
sucked downward.

I am a ballerina unwound,
a piggy bank shaken upside down.
I do not stick around like a thread caught
on a nail in the stairwell. I am gone.
Nothing, no one left.

Dead girl walking can finally rest.

A HAUNTED HOUSE BUT ALL OF THE ACTORS HAVE READ MY POETRY – Prudence Brooks

So it is not built in a home but in a hospital. They strip-search me at the entrance and force a flimsy robe over my head as someone reads my medical charts over the intercom.

Bipolar Type 1 with psychotic features.
Patient presents with general paranoia and distrust of authority.

I glance around, and every doctor is my father with a needle; every nurse is my mother flicking a syringe. I dash towards the exit, but they have removed my shoes in favor of baby blue socks that don't fit.

Patient may require a sedative.
Involuntary treatment is acceptable in case of emergency.

There is a palm wrapped around my wrist, there are tightening tendrils across my chest, and I feel a pinch. Suddenly everything begins to ooze, the walls melt into a pool at my feet and I splash around in the off-white tiles. I am used to the feeling of eggshells beneath my feet. everywhere I look, there are carnival mirrors, reflecting all the horrors in my closet. Every breakup, every bruise, every abuse inflicted on me when I was three years old, and then I see myself currently:

Age: 26 years
Height: 5 feet 6 inches
Weight: too heavy to bear

The floor spins, and I am alone in a small, cold room. There is a mat on the ground, and the walls are white. I don't have to look; I know there is a guard outside the door with his thumbs in his vest. I've been here before.

Patient intoxicated on arrival.
Patient suicidal: should be monitored closely.

Suddenly the lights go down and I am sleepy, I am so sleepy. What is this fog?

Take twice a day with or without food.
May cause side effects.
Oh right, that's how this ends. That's how this always ends. With a swig of room temp water and giving in. With a certain dimming. So why wouldn't this tour be the same? Why wouldn't the grand finale be a sixty-day prescription

and a light turned off?

"I do not stick around like a thread caught on a nail in the stairwell. I am gone. Nothing, no one left."

- Prudence Brooks

2 a.m. Thoughts

more jumbled than the
buttons in my bedside table:

There's a shadow that follows,
lurking in the corners
of my room, whispering,
"You don't really deserve this."
"You didn't really earn it."

and I bury my head in a blanket.

A worn-out candle flickers,
struggling as it slowly consumes itself,
leaving behind a moment
of smoke,
then darkness

and a hard puddle of wax
to clean up tomorrow.

The morning is on its way
but Witching Hour comes first;

So, I collect my buttons and
pay my mourning dues.

- **Bea Cardella**

The little monster
in my chest
has been ignored
for the last 5 days:

There's too much to do,
family to see,
gifts to exchange.

The feelings I suppress;
he gnaws on them in my
negligence, growing bigger
and restless, thrashing
inside his cage of bone.

He claws
against my sternum, tearing into the mallow.
I will have to cancel my
plans today; take the time to
tame this terrorist
      give him water
      give him sun
      a guided meditation to focus on-
he does not relent.
In tears, I will find myself
tonight on the floor—
my lover's warm palm
pressing against the monster's dwelling,
his hand rising and
falling with the rhythm
of our shared breaths.
He does not reprimand the beast—he gives it a kiss.
I'll rest my head
against his shoulder
and the monster will sigh
and curl up for the night.

           Tomorrow, it will start again.

-   **Bea Cardella**

"He does not reprimand the beast— he gives it a kiss."

- *Bea Cardella*

Pine Needles – Edsard Driessen

Overflowing
Inanimate,

Choking on the glass noose,
As that purple ooze
Drips down the walls,

She snatches at the clay on her top lip,
Smearing the red on the cotton lining of
A velvet top.

Does no one ever notice (how
the skirting board is always wonky)

the cabinets lean drunkenly
and the top of the ironing board stays perched
on birds' legs?

At around half past twelve
The sun stands to attention
And greets rolling hills
Green with ambition,
Brown with envy
Yellow with hurry and red with decay.

She told me her dreams had died there
Drowning in rivers
Murdered amongst the pines,
Triple homicide between the peaks.

Hitchhiking from her imagination.
Sinking beneath the expectation and the realisation.

Clasped hands hold sunken treasure,
Veins run tender stems towards rooted home,

The minute hand stretches itself awake,
hands unfurl, slinging knuckles
like a kite in a hurricane.

Another purple droplet shears itself from her lips In
between the gaps of her teeth,
nestled between lies, half-truths, and open invitations.

Her complexion seemed lacking,
Dutiful skin stood to attention
against the layout of her skull,
Sharp cheek bones
intersected deep eye sockets

like coarse pebbles on a busy driveway
Her voice rose above that dreary mist.
Cutting sideways against the bark
On which her body stayed still,
As the pine needles tattooed
Dreams onto her skin.

Brutalist Heaven – Edsard Driessen

Is there a god?

and

If there is

       Does
           He
               See
                    The
                         Man
                             Sat

On the last

Step

Of Oxford Circus?

Gazing upwards to the heavenly abyss of
hurried, faceless figures
Glancing eye-contact, hurried, hurling expressions onto white
ceramic brick.

Dead locked jaw, into the promised land beyond the crusty
white surgical lamp lighting the staircase.
Already
Dead.

G   a   z   i   n   g

Hopeful of the impossible.
Deciding whether to go right or left.

Every footfall landing repentance.

And in those same baleful eyes

We all become his God,

Take our hand,

and

> We'll

> > walk

> > > you down

while roses fall from our thorny crown.

From this brutalist heaven.

"The minute hand
stretches itself awake,
hands unfurl, slinging
knuckles like a kite in a
hurricane."

- Edsard Driessen

**Remembering (What I Wish I Would Forget) –
dsb.poetry**

sitting on a beach of
broken glass grains that
dig in deeper with
each breath inhaled.

tides are overtaken
by the black stain
of past trauma that
blew away innocence like
violent tornadoes,
rolling like a corpse
in the grave,
forgotten through years
of withering away.

eyes close,
longing & regretful,
welling, yet continuously
pushed down,
blocked by shame &
every wrongdoing listed
under my name.

planes crash &
towers burn, tainting
the skyline with
rich black plumes,
clouds of desolate hopelessness.

there's no discernible sun

on this beach of sorrow.

throat chokes back
blood, but it just
keeps coming,
& before I know it,

I've drowned,
suffocating
in all of this.

Raining Embers – dsb.poetry

autumn,
        walking.

the sun is setting
behind me,
detonating the skyline
into some
orange-purple
burst.

the wind blows
from right to left,
stripping a wall of
birch, maple, & other
trees,
raining embers
of a year's life,

orange,
        yellow,
                red.

it's a feeling
I so closely know
these days.

Ten Minutes – dsb.poetry

the eyes no longer
blink,
the legs no longer
chase,
the hands no longer
fight,
the heart no longer
beats —

ten minutes
alone with the body,
a deep, heavy stream of
memories floods through your
veins.
it's not the first, but
another one of many lost.

no matter how much you
shake, how much you
scream, how much you
beg, it just

tears
     you
         up

inside.

Salt Ain't Sugar – B. Elae

May you never
end the day
with the belief
that you aren't
worthy of the fight,
or a love without wonder
And may you always
know the difference
between being showered
in love...and being pulled under.

The Ways We Rise – B. Elae

Perhaps we
rise differently…
Them like the sun,
you like the moon,
and me like the sea.
Each resilient in their
very own form, and a
victor above adversity.
By chance, if we ever meet
in passing, let us nod
in recognition.
More for honor, instead
of competition.

Runaway Child – B. Elae

One way ticket,
runaway child,
to ease my soul
just for a while.
To find a moon that
loves me unabridged,
to see a world and feel alive.
With unharmed seas
and fresh, sweet air
to put away with every care.
To watch a sunset
and, too, the sunrise
Oh, to see a world...to feel alive.

"May you always know the difference between being showered in love and being pulled under."

- *B. Elae*

New Pen – Steven Fortune
(after William Carlos Williams)

A new
good pen
is like a fresh
stylus on a phonograph
or a stinger
in the yellow blare of
dandelion purity

So much depends
upon
it

I Savored Silence - Steven Fortune

I savored silence
like the last bite
of black forest cake

Now that I am hungry
I wish it were the voices
I had savored

Education - Steven Fortune

The brittle yellowed pages
of your lost school of thought
flutter 'round me
falling where they may
and all I can do is pray
for none to martyr themselves
to the sole flame lit in memory
of when the colleague wasn't yet
aware of student status
out of earshot

Damn It - Steven Fortune

I'd rather hear a sigh
of concession telling me
that it will happen again
than a confident conveyor
of insistences that it will not

EGGS DON'T CRACK – Haley Guthrie

when snakes
mouth them
gently violent
losing myself
unknowingly too
late, gone now.

SEASONED – Haley Guthrie

wither is the most
precious weathering
as it is so slow
you can watch
brittle, then break.

FUTILE – Haley Guthrie

i plucked my brain,
pickled regret,
a single candle vigil
outside a home i
can't come back to.

War is a Cruel One – Brittany Hancz

She takes and deceives
and decides what to leave.
Men ask for mercy,
but none truly survive,
for the dead are gone and living can't thrive.
Loved ones are left picking up the pieces
and saving the lost.
Breathing men are drowning and hearts turn to frost.
For this world is a cold one,
for both the lost and the found,
returned men now being saved as they drown.
We cling tight to what's left of them,
for they're withering away.
War is a cruel one,
but she will not have the final say.
We'll fight together to pull the nightmares away.
Lost are our drowning brothers, sisters, parents,
daughters, and sons.
But this is not the end of their story.
They will soon see the effects
of a returned-home glory.
And we'll dance and celebrate together,
for war made us stronger.
Until then, fight on
brothers, sisters, fathers, and mothers.

Open wounds weep from the past - Jacqueline Hird

The parallel lines scream
at me from their

...jagged edges.

I remember and submit
to the hot knife that cuts
through buttery skin.

It opens the flesh but it cannot
clear the wound. Deeper it goes
with intricate cuts that are set to

...exorcise the past.

Release the frustration
and watch as it seeps
from the depths. Treacly
and thick smearing
the clean crispness of the day.

Weeping into the floor
my screams are smothered

...in silence.

Echoes of Darkness Kill the Inner Child - Jacqueline Hird

Tonight, the bent-fingered demons
crept through my window
-**cracks**.
They clambered onto my clammy skin
and with every in-breath they sank deeper
-**within,**
into my chest. Their blackened nails
-**scar**.
Prised open the fault line on my heart.
Inside a silvery pearl of hope
sat in silence desperately trying to hang on
-**deeply**
but the sharpness speared her
-**forever**
and veins of despair ate away the light.

Delivered to the Wrong Address - Jacqueline Hird

Deflation of the body looks like exhaustion,
the type where I could zip off my skin
and it would fall in a sorry heap
at the bottom of the bed. My bones complain
at me as I lift my leg with my hand coaxing
it to claim the sheets. But the duvet is heavy
and it pushes the breath from my lungs
so I lay like the roadrunner flattened;
two dimensional. Is this what it's like to see me
when I am laden with the bass notes
sent from the past to remind me exactly what I am.

A child whose skin pricks as dark moods arrive
from around corners. Whose breath moistens
the purple bedspread as she picks off the threads
in the hopes it will distract the noise.
The child with a gut full of anxious
that needs to pour out with sweaty certainty.
A scared child watching out the window,
staring at the patch of road lit by the lamp,
waiting for you to return
so she did not have to guard her fear anymore.
One who scrabbles up the stairs wondering why
those red colours fly from your face and feet
landing before she reaches the top.

I'm tired. Let me coorie up in an armchair
that is rocked by the arms of a strong man
who tells me I am a lace tied parcel

delivered to the wrong address.

An ache for that sits
like a concrete block on my chest

"Veins of despair ate
away the light."

- *Jacqueline Hird*

Loan-Doubt – Timothy Imbriglio-Roy

I didn't give up, I just put you down.
I miss your smile, why do I frown?

I can't do this, I am moving on.
Find me passed out, on the lawn.

No love lost, I had given.
I have to go, find my own heaven.

I don't know, why you do this.
Retrace your steps, watch your movements.

I was alone, cold and tired.
You brought me in, next to the fire.

Days with you, we had the best time.
Now I think, can these memories be mine?

Turn the music up, in the car.
If you love me, it will go far.

Feel the rhythm, it gets faster.
I know this feeling can last here.

(Unrefined song lyrics for "Watch your Movements" by No Detour)

Turned to Dust – Ghada Khalil

Dreams bright as stars fade,
Turned to dust, lost to time's grasp.
Memories linger,
Hopes fading in the wind's sigh,
Gone with the passing of time.

Drown Me in Your Gaze – Ghada Khalil

Drown me in your gaze, so deep and true,
Where oceans of emotions ebb and flow.
In the depths of your eyes, I find my peace,
Lost in the currents of your soul's release.

Engulf me in your eyes, a tranquil sea,
Where waves of passion crash upon the shore.
In the stillness of your gaze, I find my rest,
Submerged in the depths of love's eternal quest.

Drown me in your gaze, my heart's desire,
Where every glance ignites a sacred fire.
In the infinity of your eyes, I find my truth,
Immersed in the essence of eternal youth.

Thank God for Angels – Ghada Khalil

I walk the earth with arrogance and pride,
Greed is my middle name, all for me or none at all.
Envy pours from my pores,
My soul lights with fire, passion for lust,
Unsatisfied gluttony, my body's playground.

Feed me, mind and soul, never enough,
Sloth over worship, let me be,
Or face my wrath, thank God for angels,
Holding back the seven buried sins within.

Hunger - Sasha Kolossovsky

I imagine your lust for me would be like a spiderweb
Delicate shining threads
wrapped along where your fingers trace
My skin melts under their touch
The air pulses with my heartbeat
Time slows
Until the thumping in my ears is all that's left to remind
me time exists at all
I can feel your heart too
See the hunger in your eyes
Experience the urgency in your touch
The last of my breath floods from my parted lips
I'm hungry too.

Sweet but not ripe - Sasha Kolossovsky

I hope my father feels the weight
of my youth on his shoulders
That he sucks every drop of my innocence down
I hope the sticky sweet childhood of mine
Mine but never mine
Bubbles in his stomach
Churning like an unruly sea
Meets grief for the daughter that he could have had
Adulthood is mine, all mine
and becomes acid
I hope it eats him from the inside out

ache – Jordyn Krieg

We are mangled by gentle hands
to be something other than the
anything we are meant to be.
We are tiny, beautiful bonsai trees.
Bent and broken and fond of the
knots that tied us together in early
March on top of the washer in the
basement of your college dormitory.
I've tried being a doormat; I just
prefer lover instead, even when my
heart aches with the guilt of undeserving.
With recollections of draped mirrors
and reminders to be unkind to myself.
With memories of being cruelly loved.

It still hurts when you look at me like
I'm not the worst decision you ever made.

traffic light intersections - Jordyn Krieg

I never asked you
your favorite color,
probably because
I figured that wasn't
the sort of thing
you would bother to have.
I never asked you
about a lot of things,
but we went on
three dozen silent car rides
together and I'd count
the number of times
you breathed between
traffic light intersections.
Sometimes,
I think we hear more
without conversation.
Sometimes,
I think words
can ruin a person.

cover our hips with tattoos - Jordyn Krieg

We write love letters to
our acne scars and apologize
to our wrists for all the
crescent moons that illuminated
the broken bodies
we thought we were
supposed to want to have.
We cover our hips with tattoos.
We cover our stretch marks
with pantyhose, and
cover our fingernails
with clenched fists we
throw only at ourselves.
We cover our arms with flowers.
Who says the breaking
cannot be beautiful?

the throes of good love - Jordyn Krieg

In the throes of good love,
everything in poetry.
I know it spelled out in
beads of sweat on the
nape of your neck as
you're sleeping belly down
on the bed and I know it
when I see my
blood-stained panties
mingling in a pile of
our dirty laundry on the floor.

"Sometimes, I think words can ruin a person."

- *Jordyn Krieg*

A Promise Sturdier Than Silver – Selene Ceridwen Lee

And that will be justice
On a Tuesday afternoon when we are both tired,
But not of each other,
Never of each other.

We will smile and touch in small pauses, delicate places,
ungently.

The world will look on,
Just another pair of people that know what it means to
ache too well.
They do not know the way we choose each other;
Not in spite of flaws, but because of them
Though in spite of rationality.

I will circle you like the moon, milky and beaming.
Be my center and I will be yours,
A promise sturdier than silver bands for it comes more
from our servant hearts than law.

That will be justice
When I call you mine and there will be no need to look
back,
I'll walk right beside you and purposefully bump at your
shoulder.

In My Dreams – Allie Linn

My lungs burn, my legs ache
Sweat trickles down my back
The sun reflects brightly off the fresh snow
You stride towards me and smile

You hike at my pace, easy conversation flows
It feels like we could do this forever
But I'm aware we're running out of time
You smile at me and say my name

The scene blurs as I awake
And just like that you're gone

The Spark of Danger – Allie Linn

A teasing glance
Liquid courage
Time stands still
Signs of danger ignored
Butterflies
Sides chosen
Narcissistic web woven
A look was all it took
Disbelief that you chose me
Naive to what comes next

Twins - Gwendolyn Meredith

I saw my twin,
Walking down the street of New Orleans.
She was tall, proud, with flowers anointed,
Her curved, thick trunk, a sign of pride, stability,
Her many branched limbs the picture of gracility.

She was slowly escaping, breaking free
Of the concrete constraints at her feet.
Roots curling up, pushing back persistently
Against unnatural barriers laid by humanity.

One day, I have no doubt,
We'll finally break out.

Balance - Gwendolyn Meredith

A rainbow does not dream of yellow days,
Seeking out only those sunny golden rays,
Push away blues, or run from harsh truths.
Slice out pieces of itself, weeding away
Until the garden is barren.

Instead,

She gives equal space to all of colors
Casting their radiance across the sky,
never diminishing one for another.
Seeking the beauty in all shades of light,
Finding none more deserving than the rest.
A rainbow is confident in all parts of herself,
which may be the secret I should mirror myself.

Wholeness - Gwendolyn Meredith

Sometimes I hold my own hand
As memories pass, waves on sand.
My mind shifts through the moments,
Weaving them together, making sense.

I watch the waves come and go,
Feelings rise up and I know
These aren't me, but they fill me
Consuming, I grip my hand. Breathe.

Anger, jealousy, rage, shadows
Lurking in the dark, yet not our foes.
My young mind shrinks in fright.
While I welcome the exiled sight.

Since I've learned to hold on,
Not allowing myself to be torn.
Watching the entire ocean's beauty,
I feel my wholeness and complexity.

Wildness - Gwendolyn Meredith

Sometimes I feel her stirring deep inside,
The women who was unable to thrive
When the girl was flayed apart by the world.
Still there is still an ancient seed burrowed.

Still her siren song lures me deep into myself,
Pulling me back to center.
To a space filled with sturdy oak trees, berries,
Winding trails with flowers by the sea.

When I loosen my grip, inhibitions flee,
I sink. She catches me.
An instinctual trust, A soothing whisper
"feel everything, run wild, and live free."

"Feelings rise up and I
know these aren't me,
but they fill me."

- *Gwendolyn Meredith*

Poison – Ophelia Monet

you think this is
what you want,
that this is
queen anne's lace
on my tongue

but my love,
it is hemlock

i am not a glowing thing—
i am poison
dressed in delicate petals

petals unfurled – Ophelia Monet

i will allow myself to bloom
into the woman
who has been stuck screaming
inside of my chest
for decades,
angry with a world that
would not let her become
the version of herself
who fights relentlessly,
petals unfurled and fuming

ephemeral – Ophelia Monet

i woke today
missing you
melancholy greeting me
the moment i
opened my eyes

dust on the windowsill
an empty glass on
the nightstand
overflowing hamper
obsidian pooling in
my gut at the sight
of each

despair,
an unwelcome guest,
the kind that invites
themselves in

eyes shut tight
a momentary pep-talk
amidst a mind in a
state of entropy
and i spiral

down
  down
    down

into this
ephemeral darkness

echo - Ophelia Monet

clouded recollections
hazy mind
uncalibrated
by grief
the loss of you

ripples in the water
are but echoes of
the past
in the same way
memories are but
a reverberation
of what once was

you are a ripple
in my mind
in my memories
causing brief havoc
at random intervals

this bed, once a haven
now only
a tarmac for my
body to land upon
and rest

shut my eyes
not even sleep
is safe from
the echoes
of you

"I am not a glowing thing— I am poison dressed in delicate petals."

- *Ophelia Monet*

Soulmate – Rayna Nisbett

God how I miss it.
How I crave you.
All I feel is black, but I admit.
I want your face to be my new view.
Wishing you were here,
Is it my fault that I want you to want me?
Why can't I go back to last year?
When you were purely in my thoughts
And I was completely free.
All I want is that one kiss.
The one where you feel sparks sizzling
through the air.
Then I could give a sigh of bliss
And not have to worry about you because
I don't want to share.
I feel nothing when I'm with the typical guy.
Is there something wrong, yes, it's just this.
I want you so bad I feel like I'll die.
All the romance in the world watches
as I fall into the abyss.
Don't I deserve a happy ending?
Where I get my one true person.
Even as I tip deeper into the ground, transcending.
You rise, and now it's determined.
I like you, I want you, I have for years.
But you're with her, and in plain sight.
I don't know why you can't confront your fears.
No idea, but now I'm alone and you will
always burn bright.

Storybook World – Rayna Nisbett

Rain, the way it fell, never ending.
Creating a storybook world, forever captivating me.
Never will I fully let go, I am descending.
Meeting you all for the first time, completely free.
Never have I laughed so much.
Never have I talked until the sun was rising.
How I miss everything, from the smell of the air, and the
views all around me.
The clothes, the people, the places
So uncomplicated, yet so rewarding.
I wish for one second, I could be back,
in the world of never-ending stories.
Suddenly, the flowers beam right at me,
early in the morning.
All I want is to roam the city before I die,
see the world in all its glory.
I miss your presence, the different stages.
How we all loved each other,
and always found our way back.
How I long to go again,
the castles beckoning to me for ages.
We will see each other again, but suddenly,
I'm falling through the sky, in a flash,
all I see is black.
Longing for the style, the buildings,
the architecture of it there.
Thrust back to reality, where chaos surrounds me, casting
a gloomy glare.
All I want is my life to be like last year.
Where we were together, and I had nothing to fear.

"All the romance in the world watches as I fall into the abyss."

- *Rayna Nisbett*

A Warm Place – Mia Pantano

I crawl into your chest and wrap myself
around your heart like a blanket
keeping it warm
the cool air makes me shiver
goosebumps up my back
my legs
my breasts
my meager body heat
keeping *you* warm
I'm safe in you
I'm real
I'm *alive*
your heart beats so strongly against my chest
I can pretend the beat is my own

Ouroboros – Mia Pantano

I bite my tongue
and blood is the first thing I taste in three days
I'm eating myself—

but I've been eating myself all along
you would think I'd be used to the taste
by now

Scientific Breakthroughs Undocumented. – Matthew Pasquarello

when the carnival is over and the tin man
goes home
to the roller coaster!
trust his rusty parts over the new ones
(graveyard)
we will hear pleasant mechanical bumps
in the night
(digging graves is for the strong-willed)
won a chess game
with the modern man,
looking out the windows better
than predecessors who at least knew how to
pour the cereal before the milk.

son-of-a-bitch
a path carved by
human feet and my
trusty mutt
not
knowing how to preserve
what we are given in a nice
wicker basket

so even if it's frosty
don't know how to
stuff a scarecrow properly. all these birds are
taking over the farm…
so let them
they're probably better with handling the money

**Bill Paxton Was Flawless In Twister. – Matthew
Pasquarello**

what was to be expected,
the fraud on the frontlines,
the cricket in the shadow of the
priceless violin

she'll let you know when she's
done with her symphony,
come pesticides or
tire treads

he'll let you know when he's
done listening to propaganda,
come a wrong turn or a
tornado warning

Part Me, Part Swindler. – Matthew Pasquarello

highway by the river polluted with irregular colors.
part anxiety-ridden man of steel
will.
part puppeteer.

mentality really jumbled its puzzle pieces,
that one day on the swingset.
rapid formative years.

kidnap your sewing kit and
create new companions.
stare at the sun when it's at its most weak.
it will blush.

pull that dress hem out of the dirt.
a normal existence wandering various hallways
can work.

paint these walls with those same irregular colors.
chop wood out in the pea-shooter
forest when duel season has come
to an end.

why worry? the world only hides in the corners
of the room when she's
planning something great.

another war, another dandelion army.
there are islands in your cuticles,
is that why you insist on being
so delicate?

sick brain sings louder than the idiot sane.
you'll believe the newspapers
when they're the only thing left.

simmer down.
speak heavily into the ears of the clouds and
they still won't grant us a snow day.
fuckin' psychopaths.

there's so many memories clowning around
in rotten fruit bowls riddling the planet's timid
ecosystem.
they are there too.

"The world only hides in the corners of the room when she's planning something great."

- *Matthew Pasquarello*

Blackhole – B. Reign

This pit in my stomach keeps growing
As I shrink deeper and deeper into myself
How small can I possibly get
Until I eat myself whole
Until there's nothing left
Of the girl I used to know

Ghost – B. Reign

Staring in the mirror
A ghost of a girl
Stares back at me
She lives outside
But she's all I see
Numb to her surroundings
No longer feeling
Because you took everything
A hostage to her being
Her home no longer hers
How does it feel
To love a ghost
That's no longer yours

Wings – B. Reign

In my cocoon nestled in
Taking my time
Healing and Resting
As flowers bloom all around
Warmth from the sun beating down
My heart is yearning
Expanding and stretching
I am ready for my wings to be found

Buoyant – B. Reign

Trying to teach my heart to swim
When all it's ever known is sinking

"How small can I possibly get until I eat myself whole, until there's nothing left?"

- B. Reign

In Another Life – Steph Sacco

Somewhere
in another life,
I am a knife.

Serious, jagged,
razor-sharp,
but still meant
to be held carefully.

Tough – Steph Sacco

I don't want to be
tough
all the time.
Just once, I want to be
the flower and
not the bomb.
A daisy or a buttercup.
A meadow of me,
blowing in the breeze.

Barefoot in spring, you
stop to admire my progress.
There is beauty
in fragility.

One step
at a time,
I tell myself.
Today, I won't wear combat boots
with my sundress.

Antipsychotics – Elizabeth Anne Schwartz

She is so clever,
and I know nothing:
I see night sky,
she witnesses death
at the heart of the star.

My flower
is her rotting seed,
gasping for breath
and choking on
morning dew.

My pills are her
arsenic,
my pleas shrill
as a fox in a trap,
while she seeks the hunter.

Salt tears on my cheeks
are nonsensical;
the bitterness
of these truths
is all she can taste.

She weaves patterns
like webs of copper:
her mind is a mirror,
reflected in a mirror,
as I sit in the dark.

Women Named Peter - Elizabeth Anne Schwartz

Did you see her, too?
On stage in her tights and charm,
feathered cap and collar,
prettiest boy alive
with a glint in her eye
that teased the thrill of never never,
double negatives
dimpling her cheeks
like the possibility of flight.
Is there a world where
we can grow down,
away from wedding lace
toward the brashness
of her stride,
boyish promises
made to lost girls—
those of us in the crowd
praying never to be found?

To Be a Bride - Elizabeth Anne Schwartz

Here is the lace,
layers of tulle to hide
that something blue,
tucked at the waist
to keep it close,
something borrowed,
swell of merit from
the faces in the crowd.

Here is the ring,
flush of sanctioned
womanhood,
something new
to try on
at the vanity,
something old
staring back
from behind mascara,
waterproof.

Confessional - Elizabeth Anne Schwartz

Forgive me, Father, for I have sinned.
In the churchyard,
when I imagined her
wearing nothing but
the cross her mother gave her.
And again, in the sanctuary,
when we kissed
and she tasted like wine,
Christ's blood on our tongues.
We broke open the apple, Father;
slid our fingers along
the seeds at its core.
Let the juice fill our mouths
and run down our chins,
licked its sweetness off our lips
like Eve so many moons ago.

Watching The Seventh Seal - Elizabeth Anne Schwartz

Max von Sydow's
jaded knight
tries to pray
to a silent God;
only Death answers.

"We broke open the apple, Father; slid our fingers along the seeds at its core."

- Elizabeth Anne Schwartz

Numb-ered Days – Cat Speranzini
(after Timothy Imbriglio-Roy)

"I miss you sometimes,"

you say, like I'm gone.
My essence in ashes, on the lawn.

I may be different than before,
but my heart still thunders

to the rhythm of your song,
you pound the drums, I sing along.

I didn't mean to lose the person I was,
my last good day a lesson in staying strong.

If you can't do this, then just move on.
I am the dark before the dawn and

you are the sun that shines so bright,
the only light in the shadow of my life.

Just forget me, I was wrong.
I thought I knew how to love,

but I am so far gone from who I was.
Still, I promised, I won't give up.

Your hope a beacon, my rage a boat
carrying us through an ocean of doubt.

A Nor'easter Hit the Night we Decided to End it – Cat Speranzini

It's late, still light pours
through the windowpanes
into the empty chambers
of my torn and bloodied heart.

Is this how love dies:
desperately thunderous,
screaming like lightning bolts
breaking apart the black sky?

I let the light pour,
watch as it devours,
whisper my goodbyes.

Once, there was a tree... – Cat Speranzini

Not sure how to tell you this, but
I loved a tree so much I ripped the bark
to shreds of paper in my hands

dry and crumbling.

Like skin peeled anxiously from around
a cut.
Like I tried so hard and eventually
gave up.

I loved a tree so much I climbed a branch
so thin it snapped beneath my feet.
I pulled off the leaves and kept them

in a diary.

Like biting my lip until
it splits.
Like scratching the same spot,
an unquenchable itch.

I loved a tree so much I cut it down,
kept the trunk a stump in the ground.
The bark was beautiful on my shelf,
so ruggedly lovely,

a decaying body.

Like a pinned butterfly
on a wall,

so pretty and so
useless now.

I loved a tree so much I couldn't bear
to let it live, kept its dissected parts
until they rotted.

Like holding on so tight and finally
letting go.
Like realizing what I loved
had choked.

Not sure how to tell you this, but
I don't love you like I did,
I held on so long

we decomposed.

Blood Rite – Cat Speranzini

Cherry apple pomegranate blushing
baby girl Barbie doll, bleeding
like you mean it.

Too rough hands, callous covered,
hairy knuckles, stubby nails coated
in flecks of red velvet cupcake.

It's papaya summers and
angel food cake until it's
rote grutze—cranberry juice
and raspberry filling

dripping from legs to fingers
to satin sheets while he turns to
the tv, controller in hand,
so he can justify watching
animated breasts on a big screen

while you re-apply
red-as-sin matte lip stain
with a cracked phone screen,
smile for the camera while he
covers his joystick in crimson
like paint.

Wear it like nail polish, don it
like armor. You are shrieking,
crossbow killing, don't-mess-with-me-ing
as he lines up a headshot,
asks the team for more healing.

A goddess coated in flakes
of scarlet, take the A on your chest
and the ruby red slippers,
click your heels and escape
the witch's pyre, this bedroom
a tomb of things he desires

and like Carrie you rise
from the blood soaked crescendo,
burn the dance floor to cinders.
No apologies for
your inherited rage,
let him incinerate

as he dodges a killing blow,
curses the game, and you
think about breaking
his Playstation, but maybe
you'll just bleed on it.

"No apologies for your inherited rage, let him incinerate."

- *Cat Speranzini*

how to exist – Kaitlyn Sun

is a question i throw to the daisies
somewhat scathingly
while they, unfazed, tilt their sunny faces
to the bright and unblinking sky.
so i offer the question heavenward
while my lips emit a sigh.
the light, airy clouds pity me
and paint a terse reply:
> *stop looking around for counsel*
> *when the answer lies inside.*
and i am once again reminded
i write in order to survive.

dark secret – Kaitlyn Sun

at the empty train station
across from the cemetery
angel numbers buzz above my head
& the haloed glow of the clock face
is a beckoning portal
whispering a dark secret
(my immortal suffering
clings to it like hope)
the metal tracks conspire
silver twins beneath the moon
(they know of my late night
conversations with a rope)
i keep it
close to my chest
like a blood-stained valentine
i repeat it
like a sermon guarding my soul
and my dark angel
begins to resemble the light.

Ondine's Curse – Kaitlyn Sun

Existing in the womb was easy
as a fruit blooming from a bough.
As soon as I was plucked from the stem
my baby skin began to sour.
       The natural instinct to live
      is not second nature to me.
Sage notes ferment into the peach flesh.
I still grapple with the lone *i* in *exist*.

desire – Kaitlyn Sun

why does this desire
to be seen
feel like a sin?
i mean it feels almost
carnal
the way i want you
to strip me with your eyes
let my defensive layers fall
like satin slipping off the skin
exposing my soul.
i want to be vulnerable.
i want to open up
spill my guts on the floor
and instead of turning
away in disgust
i want to hear you beg
for *more*.

"I still grapple with the
lone *i* in exist."

- *Kaitlyn Sun*

Curves – Ant Tellez

You've been through the
storms. You've carried yourself
with minimal ease.
It is time to walk away
from the exhaustion
as you inch closer
towards your peace.
Let the sand
blanket your travels
as you soak up
the land's natural light.
Overwhelmed by
serenity
as your greatest curve
shines so bright.

Emoji – Ant Tellez

Lifeless company,
sincere silence,
repressed emotions,
feeling mindless.
Why is it so hard
to crack a smile?
Laugh out loud
and make it
worthwhile.

Earth Angel – Ant Tellez

You're here,
I thought I lost you.
It made me so nervous
to see you vanish over time.
But here we are
reunited once again.
I'll do my best to keep you
here in a space that feels so sublime
and at times
when you must go,
I promise to remember
the moments I felt most alive.
Because of you
I know what it feels like
to have the genuine pleasure
that exists within every breath
of this life.

Warmth – Ant Tellez

I feel as much as you feel.
I ache as much as you ache.
I see the pained look in your
eyes. I know exactly what is at
stake.
I'm holding on for dear life
to this feeling we had called "forever."
Sitting and curling within
my solitude; a feeling I'm dreading
more than ever,
because your warmth is all I truly
wanted. Instead, I'm left here to freeze in
despair. Maybe someday you'll open
your arms and allow me once more
a touch to repair the aches that we feel.

"When you must go,
I promise to remember
the moments I felt most
alive."

- *Ant Tellez*

Why Not Me? – Haley Valenta

I've told this story a thousand times before
Do you think love is caught like a fish
Or is it a wish on plastic stars from the dollar store?
I stumble on the complexities
Of a hand on the small of my back
Of the intricacies of not having an anxiety attack
Just by being held
I carry my spine like an orchid
I read manuals and carry this intrepid belief
That I am unlovable
Even though I know I'm not
I see myself like tree rot
But plenty of assholes are loved
So why can't I be?
Oh yeah…
Anxiety

Door Slam – Haley Valenta

You were my most painful goodbye
Which is to say I sought after it like a caffeine fix
Or the answer to magic tricks
Or peace
Mostly peace
To rid of a defensiveness that resembled angry geese
And eyes that were red from all of the crying

Meet You There – Haley Valenta

I dreamt we talked for a while
And then I woke up
Smiling
Like car rides home as a kid
When all you see are clouds and stars and spaceships
And everything's fair
And I'm blissfully unaware of a lot of things
My dad carries me inside
Body, limp and then contracting
Dreaming of more conversations with you

Distractions – Haley Valenta

I saw it in the small things
That weren't really small
Or trivial or forgettable
When I sat and thought about it all
Because if it made me smile?
That was revolutionary
And it made me forget about the things that scared me
Like letting you go

"I stumble on the complexities of a hand on the small of my back, of the intricacies of not having an anxiety attack."

- *Haley Valenta*

**I have to hold myself back from tearing me open –
Ashley Zoro**

she looks at me
the mirror broken

claws around skin
tattered fingers
anger held in

i am the tide of doubt
under the surface
as the sea is leveled out

i expose the seams
rip the cuticles
make her bleed

punch the reflection
expose the muscle
shatter the perception

behind the glittering
here i wait

i am my own misery
the 10 foot waves

nocturnal yearnings – Ashley Zoro

a feasting of flesh as the pendulum swings
helping you learn a closer way to home

stuff flowers into your throat
say repeated pretty wordings

create smile lines
even as you're bleeding

a comfort is found in the herding of clones
an arsenal of flimsy stems and next steps

they're grinding down
your fangs with stone

but it's in your nature
the nocturnal yearnings in your bones

to rip the carotids from their necks
becoming the reaper for what they've sown

each leaf that falls is a death – Ashley Zoro

a stillborn baby,
a son getting hit by a drunk driver,
a suicide attempt.
a child being slaughtered,
a woman crying out for help
as she breathes her last breath,
a ninety-year-old man sleeping peacefully
as his soul lays to rest.

what follows is
ever permanent impermanence,
water flowing back towards the roots,
ever growing as something else is
broken into two.

so when you fall to the earth,
you're encapsulated by it once more.
dirt covers you, fills you up,
spits you back out reborn.

to *be* again
and again.
again again again.

the cycle repeats
until the sun swallows us whole.

"The cycle repeats until the sun swallows us whole."

- *Ashley Zoro*

Contributors

Zack Albertini is a writer from South Jersey. While working on his novel, he found his love for poetry, which he shares regularly on his Instagram. His writing focuses on topics of mental health, love, and introspection. When he's not writing, he enjoys spending his time playing with his two children, sipping wine with his wife, reading, or traveling. Find him on Instagram @byzackalbertini

Nataša Benedičič is from Slovenia, but has always written in the English language. She has self-published three poetry books. One of her poems was published in the Literary Revelations anthology. Find her on Instagram: at @natasek_poetry_corner

Michelle Bosonnett is an Irish writer using Instagram as her main writing space. She has been writing in various forms since childhood. Her poem "Under a Gazan Sky" was published in the inaugural publication of *Sparks Literary Journal.* Her compilation entitled "Magic in the Mundane", comprising ten poems, is currently in the process of being published by *Luain Press Publishing.* Find her on Instagram @wildflowergirl81

Morgan Bridges received her Bachelor's in English from Georgia Southern University. She has been published in the anthology *Descendants of Medusa* and *Perceptions Magazine.* Find her on Instagram: @bridges_between_worlds__

Prudence Brooks (she/her) is a poet residing in Portland, Oregon. Prudence has been writing and performing poetry since age nine and views writing as an opportunity to explore her identity as a queer, disabled woman. Prudence's work has appeared in Querencia Press, Feral Journal of Poetry and Art, Eunoia Review, Pile Press, and others. Find her on Instagram @prudence.writes

Bea Cardella has been writing stories and poems since she was seven. Her pieces use metaphor and allegory to share personal experiences in an evocative, relatable way. Find her on Instagram @beacardellapoetry

Edsard Driessen is a Dutch-raised, London-based, poet. Disturbing the grit of everyday life with the grace of the written word, he attempts to look back at the stylistic abstraction of the early 1900s and weave language into the pastiche of urban, contemporary life. Edsard is currently working towards the publication of his debut collection "*Mud*", and has been published in *Hard Magazine, The Stray* and *Viral Verses; Art in Exceptional*

Times edited by Dr. Stephen Linstead. Find him on Instagram @culturaldialect

dsb.poetry is a Pennsylvania-based poet who packs his pieces with emotion & vivid imagery based on introspection & memories. Previous publications include "We Were Fire in the Night" & "Sooner Than Forever." Find him on Instagram @dsb.poetry

B. Elae is a published author, poet, & performer from Indiana who's strived to create safe spaces through her poetry & advocacy for survivors of crime. Find her on Instagram @b.elae

Steven Fortune is a resident of Sydney, Nova Scotia (Canada) and a graduate of Acadia University (English Literature/History). He has released five poetry collections to date, edited several works for others, and has also appeared on CBC Radio, while his work has been featured and read on several radio programs. He also aspires to write for the stage, having recently completed his first one-act play. Find him on Instagram @kublakhan27

Haley Rose Guthrie lives with her husband and her one true love (her dog), Benjamin Dingo. She loves hiking and camping. She is an innovative costume creator. Halloween is life. Find her on Instagram @hg4rmthe573

Brittany Hancz is a local DFW aspiring author. Published works include "The Forest's Song," a self-published children's book. Find her on Instagram @wordswithbritt

Jackie Hird is a late blooming poet growing in confidence. She lives in Perthshire in Scotland and her writing is inspired by the challenges she faced growing up and by the time she spends in nature. Find her on Instagram @Jackie.Hird1

Timothy Imbriglio-Roy is a reader for *Grey Coven Publishing* and the drummer of the band *No Detour*. In addition to playing drums, he occasionally writes songs. He enjoys listening to audiobooks, skateboarding, and airsoft. Find him on Instagram @timmysaysskate

Ghada Khalil is a poet of thoughts and an aspiring novelist. Thus far, she has had her poetry published in literary journals such as, most recently, *Prosetrics* and *Prizzie Magazine*. Find her on Instagram @brushandpentales

Sasha Kolossovsky was born and raised in Rochester, NY. She has earned a master's degree from Daemen University's accelerated Physician Assistant program and currently works as a primary care P. Find her on Instagram @sashawritespoems

Jordyn Krieg is a poet whose emotive work speaks honestly about mental illness, body image, love, heartbreak, trauma, and her sinuous healing journey. She received a dual degree in English and History from Rider University, and self-published her first poetry collection *as endless as all things blue*. Krieg resides in upstate New York with her husband Erik and their two quirky cats, Normin and Clementine. Find her on Instagram @cleowrote

Selene Ceridwen Lee is an experimental new writer with an adoration for free verse, prose poetry and flash fiction that centers around romantic and philosophical themes. Find her on Instagram @darlinglune

Allie Linn is a dancer, choreographer, and writer. She began writing poetry when an injury prevented her from using dance as a creative outlet. Inspired by others, she aspires to publish her own book one day. Allie can often be found attending live theater and dance performances. She lives in New York City with her husband and puppy. Find her on Instagram @dancing_poetry_

Gwendolyn Meredith is a speech pathologist by day, aspiring poet by night. She is living happily with her spouse and their three lovely cats. She Embraces healing, queer love, nature, and peace through poetry. Find her on Instagram @Merediths_Poems

Ophelia Monet is an educator, mother, and storm chaser living in the suburbs of Cincinnati with her husband and their son. She began writing in 2022, after learning that her late mother was a published writer under a pseudonym. She can often be found reading a fantasy novel and wandering barefoot through forests. Her work has appeared or is forthcoming in The Malu Zine, Beyond Words Literary Magazine, Loud Coffee Press, Aureation Zine, and Blue Lake Review. Find her on Instagram @mysoullaidbare.

Rayna Nisbett is a 21 year old singer/songwriter, actress/musician, and poet from Franklin, Massachusetts. She writes poems at least once a week, and uses her real life or characters she's read about or watched as inspiration. She hopes everyone can relate to her poems, or at the very least, just enjoys reading them. She currently goes to college at Bridgewater State University, and is getting a bachelors in music. Find her on Instagram @raynanisbett12

Mia Pantano (she/they) is a writer and a dreamer. They spend their days raising a tiny human and obsessing over the nature of reality. You can find her staring into the abyss or on Instagram @evilbadmia

Matthew Pasquarello is an American writer from New Bedford, MA, known for poetry and prose. Educated at Southern New Hampshire University in Creative Writing, he has written prolifically for many years and has been published both traditionally and by self. Find him on Instagram @mpasqy

B. Reign published her first book "Chokehold" in January 2024. She is a book blogger for romance novels and thrillers @waggingwithwords and works in medicine. She has three golden retrievers and a Bernese Mountain dog. Music, tarot, reading and writing have always been her passions. Find her on Instagram @brittreignauthor

Steph Sacco grew up in Easton, Massachusetts and received her Bachelor's Degree in Creative Writing at Colby-Sawyer College in beautiful New London, New Hampshire. She's been writing seriously since high school and has been inspired even longer. Poetry is her second love after young adult fiction. She is working on her first novel. Find her on Instagram @litsandgiggles

Elizabeth Anne Schwartz (she/her) writes sapphic fiction and poetry, and loves all things dark, lyrical, and confessional. She earned her BA in Creative Writing at Purchase College. Her chapbook, *Nine Stages of Coming Out*, was recently released by tiny wren lit. Visit her website at elizabethanneschwartz.carrd.co/ and find her on Instagram @elizanneschwa

Cat Speranzini is a poet, novelist, and mother from New England. She is the editor of *Grey Coven Publishing* and a reader for *Querencia Press*. Her poetry collections "Watercolor Souls" and "Calm in the Dark" were published through *Grey Coven Publishing*. Her work has appeared in *The Eunoia Review, Moss Puppy Magazine, Glass Gates Publishing,* and *Clever Fox* amongst others. Find her on Instagram @catsperanzini.poetry

Kaitlyn Sun (she/her) is a Chinese-Australian, bisexual poet from Perth, Western Australia. She also goes by Sad Magical Girl. Kaitlyn has lived experience with mental health issues and her writing reflects on both her individual experiences as well as the broader brushstrokes of what it means to be human. Find her on Instagram @sad.magical.girl

Ant Tellez writes poetry as a source of personal therapy. He works in human resources for a university and his hobbies are writing, reading, and sketching. He is an avid music, basketball, and film enthusiast. He hopes that his writing inspires others to take the leap towards artistic enrichment. Find him on Instagram @theamorant.writing

Haley Valenta is a writer from Wisconsin. She graduated with a degree in Public Relations and Writing. Her self-publications are "When No One Was Listening" and "Wallflowers," which are available through Amazon. Find her on Instagram @hlylauren

Ashley Zoro is a writer and poet hailing from sunny Florida. With a passion for exploring the depths of the human experience, her evocative writing invites readers to journey with her into the profound introspections of the soul, the shadow and light of inner worlds, reflecting the raw emotions that resonate within us all. Find her on Instagram @amzwrites